The Monterey Bay Aquarium stands as a "window to the bay," showcasing the hidden beauties of one of the world's richest marine environments.

The living waters of Monterey Bay, the heart of our nation's largest marine sanctuary, brim with stories of life and death, growth and change.

Some have been told a million times, others we've only begun to learn.

The stories start with the place.

In rocky areas along the edges of the bay, forests of giant kelp stretch from seafloor to surface.

Three hundred feet deeper lie cold granite reefs, draped with clusters of flowerlike animals.

Elsewhere, vast sandy plains stretch from the shores to the dark depths.

In outcrops of shale, clams drill caves into the flat reefs.

High above, sleek fishes race through the open waters while delicate jellies drift with the currents.

Where land and water meet, creatures fall under the sway of the tides. Wharf pilings are draped with sea life.

And on the rocky shores, life thrives as waves crash down tons of water.

Halfway up the bay, Elkhorn Slough meets the sea in a mix of mud and marsh that's a haven for birds and fishes.

And at the center of it all lies a huge submarine canyon, its dark depths filled with stories still untold.

The Monterey Bay Aquarium is all about these places . . . all about the bay. Knowing the stories in our own backyard, we come to know the story of life everywhere. Come closer and see.

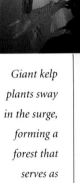

Giant kelp plants sway in the surge, forming a forest that serves as a refuge.

Monterey Bay Aquarium is perched on the southern shore of the twenty-five-mile-wide bay.

*The Monterey Bay Aquarium
is all about the bay...a stage
with a cast of thousands against a
backdrop of rocky shores, kelp
forests and the dark deep sea.*

Immense schools of squid swarm into the bay to mate and lay eggs, often ending up in nets to be sold as calamari.

The sardine industry spawned Cannery Row at the turn of the century. But the Sicilian fishermen who hauled in the "silver harvest" were only the latest in a long line of people to reap the riches of the bay.

The Ohlone people—who called the god of the bay "oh-ay-sia," the Spirit of the Holy Sea—fished here for centuries. Later, waves of immigrants—Spanish, Portuguese, Genovese, Chinese, Japanese and others—pulled their livings from the bay with ever more effective techniques.

Whales, otters, abalone and squid fell prey to these early commercial hunters. Then, with the twentieth century, came Sicilian fishermen and their efficient lampara nets. The "silver harvest" was on.

At first, the schools seemed limitless. In 1903, three thousand tons of sardines were canned in Monterey. By 1945, the catch had grown to nearly a quarter of a million tons, and Monterey had become one of the biggest fishing ports in America.

But catches began to decline in 1946, and dwindled to nothing by 1952. One by one, the canneries closed their doors. The largest of all was the last to close; the Hovden Cannery, which had anchored the row for nearly six decades, shut down for good in 1972. Its closing marked the end of an era.

But in that ending lay the seeds of a new beginning. In 1977, four biologists at Stanford University's Hopkins Marine Station proposed an aquarium devoted solely to Monterey Bay. Seven years later, Knut Hovden's old cannery was reborn as the Monterey Bay Aquarium.

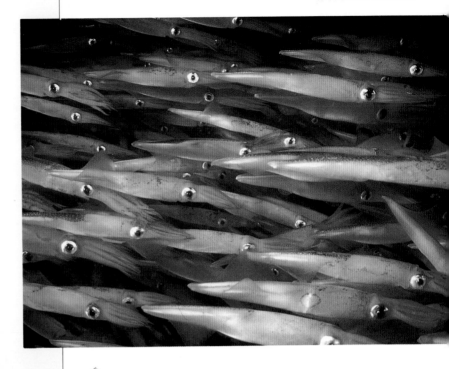

The "silver harvest" continues in Monterey Bay.

Sardines have been making a comeback in the bay.

Gone but not forgotten, the old Cannery Row lives on in paintings and photographs.

Sculpted offsite, life-size gray whale models made a brief appearance on Cannery Row on their way to the aquarium.

It took seven years to reshape the old cannery and bring the dream of a Monterey Bay Aquarium to life.

To finance the building, David and Lucile Packard made a one-time gift of fifty-five million dollars. The nonprofit Monterey Bay Aquarium Foundation was created in 1978 to oversee aquarium operations and the construction effort.

Designed by the architectural firm of Esherick Homsey Dodge and Davis to complement the style of the old cannery, the building gives visitors a sense of Cannery Row in its heyday.

The design took shape in the hands of teams of specialists who transformed the lines on blueprints into the hard steel, concrete and acrylic of complex seawater systems and giant exhibit tanks.

But even while they labored to bring the building to life, exhibit designers and aquarium staff were hard at work creating exhibits that would bring life to the building.

The twenty-eight-foot-deep Kelp Forest exhibit stands as a giant experiment in re-creating a living kelp forest.

The aquarium and bay meet in the Great Tide Pool, where artificial rocks mix with real ones. The pool is open to the tides, so wildlife freely comes and goes.

Each aquarium exhibit holds a living world. And from rearing orphaned sea otter pups to foiling an octopus's escape, much more happens than meets the eye to keep these worlds alive.

Aquarists maintain order here. They clean and collect, treat and feed, study and stock—all creatures come under their care.

But first the creatures must come to the aquarium.

Collecting means catch as catch can. With gentle touch and expert methods, the art is to bring them back alive—healthy new residents of the aquarium community.

In deep water and on rocky shores, by line, by net, by trap and by hand; the where and how of collecting varies as widely as the creatures caught.

Carefully placing anemones on rocky perches, an aquarist stocks an exhibit.

A few of the methods most visitors would never suspect. Artificial rocks set in the bay grow thick with marine life. Then they're retrieved by divers and placed in an exhibit.

Otters come here as orphaned pups, often separated from their mothers by storms.

Some creatures come on their own. Otters and seabirds visit the Great Tide Pool. And the spores of seaweeds and larvae of animals drift in with the seawater, then settle down, carpeting exhibits with changing tapestries of life.

To make all of these varied creatures feel at home, fresh seawater—the aquarium's lifeblood—flows through the exhibits, pumped in at up to two thousand gallons per minute.

Sixteen-foot-tall acrylic windows in the Kelp Forest exhibit are more than seven inches thick and eight feet wide, designed to withstand a water pressure of one hundred thirty-four thousand pounds each.

hen feeding an
opus, sometimes
ere's not a dry eye
the house.

Bright garibaldis defend their turf in the kelp forest (left), while tightly knit schools of fish (below) patrol the surface waters.

rs handfeed fish clean the Kelp Forest bit, while specially ned aquarium guides questions from us visitors.

Towering forests of swaying kelp grace the sunlit waters along the coast. And like redwood forests on land, these groves of giant kelp are lands of plenty, sheltering many in a shelterless sea.

Growing from tangled holdfasts anchored to rocks, the giant plants reach twenty, thirty, a hundred feet high, at times growing nearly a foot a day. Flat blades and bobbing floats spread across the water in a canopy pierced by sunbeams slanting down toward the seafloor.

One grove stands apart from the others. The Kelp Forest exhibit, the aquarium's centerpiece, looks so natural many believe they're looking through a window to the bay.

It's an illusion designed for both visitors and kelp.

The exhibit opens to the sky, and the sunlight streaming majestically through the amber fronds helps the kelp grow.

Pumps push up to three thousand gallons of seawater a minute through jets placed to generate natural currents in the exhibit. And the kelp here sways in a surge—vital to the plants—created by a special wave machine.

Like the wild forests, the exhibit changes with each passing season. The kelp grows in spring, then dies back in winter. What stays constant is the haven.

Amid the waves, amid the change, the forest stands serene.

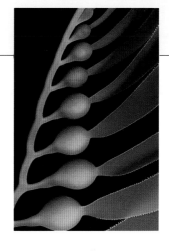

The giant kelp in our exhibit grows at the same rate as kelp in the bay, according to our in-depth studies of kelp forests.

Fields of flowerlike pink strawberry anemones are really colonies of animals that multiply by dividing in two.

From its base on the rocks to its broad canopy above, the kelp forest provides homes for the hundreds. They come in all shapes and sizes, from the gray whales who sometimes pass through to tiny hermit crabs on the seafloor below.

The Kelp Forest exhibit presents the grand vista, a sweeping overview of a cathedral-like kelp grove.

The Kelp Forest gallery on the second floor reveals more intimate landscapes. In these exhibits, visitors get a diver's eye view of a kelp forest.

Gaudy turban snails and amber kelp crabs amble up and down the giant kelp's blades and stipes. And down where the plants anchor to the rock, brittle stars and crabs squeeze into the tangled holdfasts.

Thickets of seaweeds carpet the rocks. Under them, a low-lying turf of red algae adds hiding places for crabs and kelpfishes, wizards at remaining unseen.

The Kelp Lab takes visitors even deeper into the forest.

Here, you can feel the smooth softness of a kelp frond or the leathery back of a gumboot chiton. Or discover the citrus smell of a sea lemon nudibranch, and the clever disguise of a decorator crab.

Aquarium guides, trained to interpret marine life, encourage a sense of wonder and discovery.

Microscopes and magnifying glasses bring hidden wonders to light in the Kelp Lab.

The sea slug Melibe *traps sm kelp-crawling animals in its large ho*

A sarcastic fringehead glares from its wharfside home — a discarded bottle.

You might be seeing red or orange, but along deep rocky reefs, this canary rockfish would fade to gray in the lack of sunlight.

From the deep reefs to the wharves jutting from shore, the bay's a patchwork of habitats.

For the creatures of the bay, home is where the habitat is.

Clouds of rockfishes float over the deep reefs, ready to vanish between rocks carpeted with ghostly white anemones when larger predators arrive.

Flatfishes lie half-buried in the sandy seafloor around the reefs, while sea stars trek across the open plains.

Clams and date mussels burrow through the soft shale reefs, opening up new territory for other tunnel dwellers.

Closer to shore, hungry surfperches swarm around the wharves, picking barnacles and mollusks from among the soft masses of tunicates, gaudy feather worms and twisted tubeworms ringing the pilings.

Creatures from all these communities share the Monterey Bay Habitats exhibit.

The habitats blend together here just as they do in the bay. Rocky reefs tower over patches of sand broken by outcroppings of shale.

And at one end stand pilings from an old Monterey wharf, still encrusted with twenty-year-old anemones, barnacles and tubeworms.

Between the pilings swim perch and rockfishes, while above the reefs and sand cruise sharks and salmon, striped bass and mackerel.

Restlessly roaming the bay, they weave together the habitats, linking the living communities beneath the waves.

Surfperches hang around pilings thickly encrusted with anemones, tunicates, barnacles and other prey ripe for the picking.

Sharks and schools of jack mackerel swim inches away from your nose in the Monterey Bay Habitats exhibit.

Biggest star on the coast, the platter-size sunflower star starts with five arms and adds more as it grows.

A leopard shark's mottled pattern makes it harder to see as it glides through kelp.

Sluggish horn sharks rest or crawl along the bottom.

Saving an ill or injured shark can take a surgeon's touch.

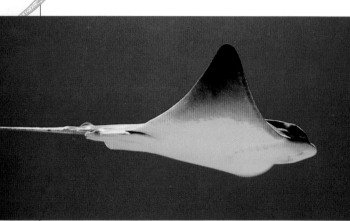

Gliding through mid-water, winding their way among rocks or lying quietly on the seafloor, sharks and rays belong to the living bay.

You can meet some of them in the Monterey Bay Habitats exhibit—a ninety-foot-long tank designed with sharks in mind.

The exhibit's hourglass shape gives sharks room to turn, and a long straight run they can cross in an energy-saving glide.

Look for large sevengill sharks and smaller sixgill and leopard sharks cruising the straightaway.

What keeps them from eating the other fishes? We keep them well fed.

Surprisingly, they don't eat as much as you might think.

Leopard sharks and dogfish get pieces of smelt or other fishes twice a day.

The larger sevengills have slower metabolisms. They're fed pieces of salmon (clipped to a long pole) once or twice a week. We've found that sevengills go through cycles where they feast one week, then nibble the next. Ongoing research gives us clues to sharks in the wild.

Some people see sharks as fearsome predators. But as we learn more about them, our terrible fascination turns to respect and wonder.

Bat rays "fly" through the water on winglike fins.

Growing to nine feet or more, sevengill sharks tend to dominate their exhibit mates.

Beautifully adapted to life in the sea, sharks are efficient predators but now risk being over-hunted.

Hardly a wolf, not really an eel, this fierce looking wolf-eel spends the day quietly in a cave, wriggling out at night to feed.

Hydrocorals grow on the reef like a small, stony forest. A vivid sea star blends right into the riotous seascape.

Eighty million years ago the bay's rock shuddered and shook; granite reefs pushed up to tower over the rocky floor.

Today the deep reefs loom over a sandy plain in the cold, dark waters a hundred to four hundred feet deep.

The Deep Reefs gallery transports you to this little-known world.

Here, the dark rocks are dotted with color. Blue sponges and orange cup corals flourish. Pillarlike white anemones stand ghostly in the faint light.

To survive here, animals hide, use disguise or flee.

Search the shadows of an exhibit for large wolf-eels and lingcod lurking among the rocks. These predators wait, as they would in the wild, for prey to stray near.

Nearby, gangly spot prawns line rocky ledges, ready to slip back into safe crevices when larger animals approach.

Wary sculpins hug the rubble, their blocky bodies blending with the rocks. Their camouflage works—as long as they sit still. Watch awhile, and you're likely to see a mottled rock scoot off to another resting place.

Even bright colors can be surprising disguises. The reds and yellows of rockfishes fade to gray in the dim light.

There's a constant feast on the deep reefs. And you can catch the flavor of life in this twilight world in the Deep Reefs gallery.

Thousands of tiny tube feet carry a giant sea star over the trunk of a hydrocoral.

*A foot
octopu
past gr
white anen
carpetir
deep*

*Profiles in camouflage,
sandy seafloor residents blend
in for protection.*

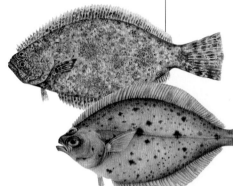

At first glance, the sandy seafloor seems barren. But dig deeper. Hidden treasure—a richness of life—lies buried in the open plains.

Where currents shape shifting patterns in the coarse sands nearshore, you'll find animals able to make a go against the grains.

The dark, still depths offshore are home to creatures who can cope in a world that's more mud than sand.

The seafloor characters change from nearshore to far; but you can meet them all in the Sandy Seafloor gallery.

Here, waving arms point out the homes of the stars. Piles of brittle stars wave their flexible arms in the water to snare passing bits of food.

The crabs in the exhibit next door don't need to dig in. Their armored shells protect them as they scuttle across open, sandy plains.

Quick-change artists, flatfishes match their color to their background. They hide where there's no place to hide by lying low and blending in.

How many flatfish can you find? Just when you think you've seen them all, a bit of seafloor swims off in search of lunch.

Sand dollars spend their lives here, too. Standing on edge, half-wedged into sandy pockets, they trap bits of food or grab small prey drifting on the currents.

Anemones and sea pens root their tubes deep in the sand. With flowing tentacles or feathery "branches," they gather prey as it brushes by.

Seek the treasures of the seafloor; these flatlands are home to living gems.

*Sea pens root deep
in the sand and
sweep the currents
for food.*

A hermit crab is always on
the lookout for a larger cast-off
shell to claim as home.

Wriggling brittle stars sometimes hide all
but their waving arms in the sand.

Short spines cover the
hard shells of living
sand dollars nestled
into the sand.

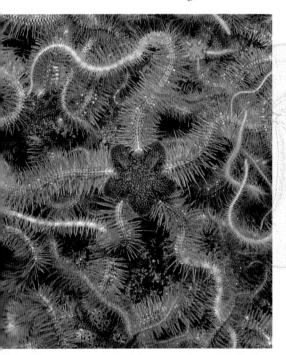

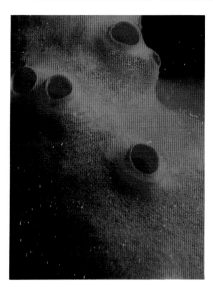

Fields of living color paint the rocks, from a brilliant sponge (above) to cobalt-blue sponges, orange cup corals and pink coralline algae (below).

Its shell covered with coralline algae, a limpet grazes on the reef's rich feast.

The shale story began thirty million years ago.

Countless one-celled plants called diatoms fell like rain on the seabed, slowly building a layer over a thousand feet thick. Time and pressure transformed their glassy skeletons into a rock called shale.

Today, the flat-topped shale reefs are honeycombed with tunnels dug by date mussels and clams that bore through the soft rock.

And once the clams dig the tunnels, all sorts of neighbors move in.

A clam's home isn't built in a day. And the artificial rocks used in many of the aquarium's exhibits won't do for residents of the Shale Reef gallery.

Exhibits here feature shale selected from the bay, and brought back with clams and other reef tenants snug in their tunnels.

Look closely. Some holes contain clams at work, their siphons drawing in food and oxygen.

Vacant tunnels become homes for others.

Small fish called fringeheads slip into the round burrows. Sea cucumbers spread feeding tentacles out of caves. And brittle stars, scaleworms and other flat animals slip through the cracks.

Creatures crowd the shale's surface, too. And floating magnifiers take you closer, revealing reef creatures' innermost secrets, like the intricate gills of nudibranchs, or the bumpy orange skin of a sea cucumber.

*Flo
magnifie
you dis
the hidden w
of a shale*

The journey from Elkhorn Slough to the ocean takes you through seven habitats: from tidal channel to eelgrass, mudflats to marsh, over the dunes and the sand beaches to the wave-swept shores.

In the aquarium's Slough gallery and Sandy Shore exhibit, you can take the same journey, without even getting wet.

These soft shores may seem lifeless at first: the salt marsh a swamp with pungent mud, the dunes deserted, the beaches lonely but for birds. Look again. They're full of life.

Clams lie stuck in the mud, siphons up like snorkels at high tide. And the burrows of fat innkeeper worms attract all sorts of lodgers.

Inside the aviary, among the fresh sea air and dunes abloom with native flowers, you'll find diving ducks, foraging sandpipers, avocets and black-necked stilts striding the shore probing for food.

Other surprises await, too. Look closely—you might discover the nest of a ruddy duck, killdeer or marsh wren.

Nearly all have been raised here from eggs. And as new broods grow, they're released to the wild.

In the slough end, leopard sharks and surfperches peer back at small visitors, beneath the paddling feet of ruddy ducks.

Past the slough and dunes, where waves wash the shore, flatfishes and guitarfishes ride the surge, or lie in wait, half hidden in the sand.

You'll find an adventure in birdwatching inside the aviary.

Beds of eelgrass conceal pipefish that hover near the blades.

A whimbrel's well-equipped probing for meals deep in the mud and sand.

An avocet and a black-necked stilt stalk the dunes.

A giant sea star closes in on a tasty limpet snack.

On the rocky edge of the bay, tides and waves rule lines of life along the crowded shores.

In zones from high and dry to low and wet, creatures live where they best can cope.

Periwinkles, limpets and a black band of algae cling to life in the highest zone, a world of sun and air: more land than sea.

Mussels, barnacles, shore crabs and rockweeds thrive in the rich middle zone between land and sea, where tides rise to cover the rocks more often than not.

Abalones, chitons and anemones stick to the low zone, full of life and only rarely exposed by ebbing tides.

The secret lives of those who live on the bay's edge open to all in the Rocky Shore gallery.

Here, monkeyface-eels wriggle between rocks where gaudy nudibranchs lay spirals of eggs.

Surfperches, at home in the perpetual motion of surge channels, turn to face currents you create with a hand-turned crank.

Turn up the currents at another exhibit and anemones open like flowers, seaweeds sway and barnacles unfurl their feathery legs. Delicate forms, they please the eye.

Theirs is a grace under pressure. They struggle to find food, defend homes and avoid predators long enough to reproduce—as waves crash and the sun blazes.

But those who contend with life on the rocky shores earn in return the sea's bounty.

A lined shore crab will use those claws when cornered, giving pause to even its largest enemies.

The bright pink sea slug, Hopkins' rose, seasonally brightens local tide pools.

Barnacles and mussels compete for space on choice tide pool rocks.

Poster-bright colors on a nudibranch broadcast a warning about bad taste or poison.

This flowerlike giant green anemone is actually an a harboring plants inside i

Rocky tide pool dwellers lead a more sheltered life than their neighbors at the shore.

Though tide pool creatures don't face total exposure or the worst of the waves, life isn't charmed. On warm days, their small seas grow saltier as evaporation begins. When it rains, the pool's diluted; their systems must handle both extremes.

Like animals everywhere, they need strategies to avoid being eaten. Tough exteriors work for crabs, while urchins and sculpins wear spines.

Crashing waves make it hard to hang on. But they also bring life: food and oxygen.

Man-made waves bring the aquarium's tide pools to life. Every forty seconds, a reservoir upstairs sends water crashing down a pipe to the tide pools below.

Enthralled by the world captured in these exhibits, aquarium explorers lean close, finding something new in each pool.

A hermit crab seeking a bigger home-shell finds one—and finds himself in a tug-o-war with another crab that wants the same shell. Peering from a crevice, a shore crab watches. When they tumble her way, she threatens both with waving claws.

Sea stars and crabs prowl the floor of the Great Tide Pool, an exhibit enclosed by rocks so natural looking few realize they're artificial.

Here, where visitors watch as baby otters learn to hunt and shorebirds comb the rocks, bay and aquarium truly meet.

*Crashing waves
every forty seconds
refresh tide pool creatures
and visitors alike.*

*Low tide leaves a bat
star high and dry.*

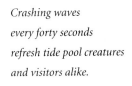

*Tide poolers discover a bounty
of sea life at low tide.*

Sea otters sometimes nap together in the aquarium's Great Tide Pool, giving aquarium visitors a chance to see these playful marine mammals up close.

The Great Tide Pool's a gathering place where visitors meet locals from the bay.

It's also a halfway house where orphaned sea otter pups learn the skills they need to return to the wild.

Our exhibit otters came to us as tiny pups, separated from their mothers. Alone, they were doomed to death by starvation.

In the early days, the goal of the Sea Otter Rescue and Care Program was simply to keep the orphans alive.

We developed special seafood "shakes" to take the place of a mother otter's rich milk. And dedicated staff and volunteers provided around-the-clock care to nurse the pups back to health.

But these otters never learned to forage for food. Unable to survive in the wild, they still live at the aquarium.

Today, pups that arrive here have a good chance of returning to the bay. From the moment pups are rescued, staff and volunteers become their surrogate mothers.

Surrogate "moms" teach baby sea otters to swim, dive and find food in the shelter of the aquarium's Great Tide Pool as a prelude to life in the bay.

They form close bonds, and the pups begin to learn. Soon, the lessons move to the Great Tide Pool. There, they learn to hunt. Their "mothers" dive for prey, crack it open, then offer it to the pups.

Later, the bay becomes the classroom.

Otters who master the lessons return to life back in the bay. The rest find homes here or at another aquarium.

Graduates of the program live around the bay today. Some still visit the Great Tide Pool.

An orphaned sea otter pup receives care and attention twenty-four hours a day

Two furry sea otters float on their backs in the water, rubbing their fur vigorously. Another finishes her meal and somersaults, to blow air into her fur.

After circling the group playfully, a male dives headfirst to the bottom of the 55,000-gallon exhibit.

Our playful sea otter pups all came to us as rescued orphans. They've never learned the hunting skills they'd need in the wild, and they're quite at home here. They romp, tumble, wrestle and carry on much like other otters in the bay.

What looks like fun is mostly serious business: in these chilly waters, otters work hard to stay alive.

All that rubbing and rolling is really good grooming: keeping the fur clean and fluffy keeps it waterproof and warm.

But even having the world's thickest fur coat can't keep out all the cold. An otter has to burn calories fast—so it eats up to a third of its weight every day.

What do we feed our frisky otters? They eat daily meals of rockfish, sablefish, squid, clams, abalone trimmings and other shellfish—and for a special treat—rock crabs several times a week.

Closely bonded to each other and their caretakers, our exhibit otters delight visitors of all ages with their antics.

Sea otters belong in the same family as badgers and weasels.

Often seen napping wrapped in strands of kelp, otters live in shallows close to shore.

Looking for more than just a snack, an otter greets its caretaker with a wet nose on the cheek.

37

Resembling fat sausages on land, harbor seals transform into sleek predators under water.

You'll find sea lions by the wharves and on some of the rocks in the bay. Sea lions can bend their hips, letting them move about on land better than harbor seals.

Seals and sea lions lead double lives. Almost perfectly at home at sea, they must seek the land each year to breed.

No seals live in the aquarium, but you can see them here every day.

Scan the water just off our decks for shy harbor seals bobbing in the water, or other perched on nearby rocks.

At times, scores of sea lions pack the rocks. When passing boats rouse them, raucous barking fills the air.

Though they look alike, with thick fur, whiskers, flippers and fat sausage-shaped bodies, seals and sea lions spring from two different families; they lead different lives.

Traits they do share show us how warm-bloods can live in the sea: big eyes and sharp hearing for dark water, where sound travels faster than in air; fur and blubber, for warmth in the chilling sea; flippers and streamlining for graceful swimming.

Adept under water, still they're linked to the land. Both bask on rocks: sea lions and elephant seals hauling out in herds, harbor seals in smaller groups.

And once a year, the ocean nomads—elephant seals and sea lions—return to traditional beaches to breed.

Twenty-three miles north, on Año Nuevo's protected shores, they crowd into rookeries. In a month-long rush, mothers bear, nurse and wean their pups, then mate again.

While on secluded beaches around the bay, harbor seals labor ashore to give birth. Mothers and pups rest there a week or so, then slip quietly into the sea.

*Harbor seals
in the bay, trac
curious gla
with visitor.
aquarium de*

Through the chill of a dense, salty ocean swim warm-blooded dolphins and whales. Mammals like us, they're so beautifully adapted to water they need never leave the sea. They surface to breathe, then dive again, to feed.

The bay's been their home for ages. Some live their lives here; others pause briefly as they roam the seas.

To see them, look to the bay.

In winter, watch for the spouts of graceful gray whales. By twos and threes, they journey south along the coast to give birth in warmer waters.

In spring, northbound mothers sometimes nurse their calves in the kelp offshore.

At other times, look for leaping white-sided dolphins or schools of boldly patterned common dolphins.

Even rarer are pods of orcas hunting seals along the edges of the bay.

To see them, look to the bay with patience and sharp eyes. But to learn their stories, look to the aquarium.

Here you can feel their presence in the lifelike, life-size models swimming overhead. Then look—listen—as labels and videos tell the tales of our ocean-dwelling kin.

Whales and dolphins call the sea home. We watch from shore and marvel at how they survive in a world so different from ours.

A spyhopping gray whale pauses for a look around.

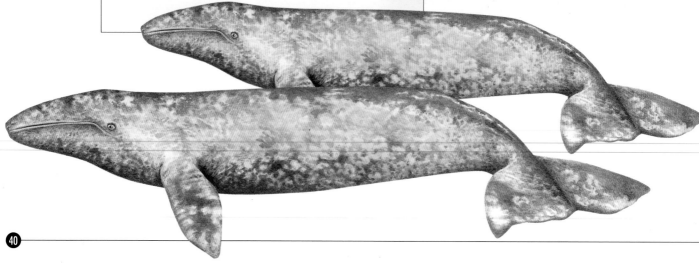

From the aquarium's decks, you can watch for the tail of a whale or other telltale signs of these coastal migrants on their journey through the bay.

Using an unmanned submersible, researchers are probing the secrets of Monterey's submarine canyon.

Scientists aboard the mother ship watch live video images transmitted from the submersible.

Beneath the surface of the bay lies a deep, dark secret: the vast Monterey Canyon.

Beginning just off Moss Landing, Monterey Canyon winds through the heart of the bay as it plunges down and out—two miles deep, sixty miles offshore.

In the frigid darkness live strange and marvelous animals, at home in a world as alien to us as outer space.

Scientists at our sister institution, the Monterey Bay Aquarium Research Institute—along with others around the bay—work to pierce the darkness.

They plumb the canyon using an unmanned submersible to extend our senses where we can't easily go.

With high-tech sensors and high-resolution video, they've begun to piece together the puzzles of life in the deep.

They've discovered a world of delicate siphonophores—deadly mid-water predators. Fishes who make their own light to lure prey—or fool predators. And gardens of clams living on gases seeping from the canyon floor.

Aquarium visitors can join in the discoveries. Each week, the sub's missions are beamed here as part of "Live from the Deep Canyon."

Still a world of mystery, the Monterey Canyon has become a living laboratory, a place where we can look and learn…a window to the deep sea.

In "Live from the Deep Canyon" visitors see what the submersible is exploring as it happens.

The Monterey Canyon rivals the Grand Canyon in scale, but few even know it exists.

A young deep sea filetail catshark thrives in the cold, dark depths of the bay.

POINT LOBOS

M B A R I

Tethered to its mother ship, the submersible begins its descent into the canyon that lies just offshore.

The Monterey Bay Aquarium seeks to tell the stories of life in the bay.

But the larger stories have yet to be told. They lie hidden in the distances of the outer bay, in the depths of a dark canyon.

Where the vastness of the open ocean and deep sea touch the edges of the bay, they forge a link between us and the two largest, and least known, habitats on Earth.

These stories reveal the inner workings of the bay and the world beyond.

The starring roles belong to the smallest creatures: the plankton—tiny, drifting plants and animals.

In their multitudes, they become pastures of plenty, nourishing all the creatures of the sea.

Transparent jellies harvest them with stinging tentacles. Vast schools of anchovies swim, mouths agape, straining them from the sea.

They fall prey to larger fishes. Slab-sided ocean sunfish lie on the surface, drifting with the jellies they eat.

By night, others rise from the depths to reap the bounty of the surface waters.

These are the stories the aquarium seeks to tell in the new exhibit wing.

When finished, the new wing will fulfill the aquarium's goal to tell the stories of all the bay's habitats.

In showing the links that connect all ocean life and by increasing our knowledge of life in the bay, the new exhibit wing will become a place to dedicate ourselves to the stewardship of Monterey Bay, and all the waters of our ocean world.

Open ocean sunfish (l[...] and blue sharks (righ[...] someday call the aquar[...] new exhibit wing[...]

Moon jellies [...] and drift th[...] the open sea [...] specially des[...] aquarium exh[...]

Behind the scenes, aquarists learn the art of making animals from worlds without edges feel at home.

"In my long life, I've never been able to see what's down there. Now, at last, all of us can. I just hope you all love it as much as I do."
— Lucile S. Packard
1914–1987